HE Dressed Me

From Stripped and Ashamed to Power

Carmenia Victoria Grant

Mike Prah LLC

Mike Prah LLC

Copyright © 2024 by Carmenia Victoria Grant

All rights reserved. No part of this book may be reproduced in any form without the permission of the author, Carmenia Victoria Grant.

Scripture quotations taken from the Holy Bible, New International Version (NIV). Copyright © 1973, 1978, 1984, 2011 by Biblica, Inc.™. Used by permission. All rights reserved.

Scripture quotations taken from the Holy Bible, New Living Translation (NLT). Copyright ©1996, 2004, 2007 by Tyndale House Foundation. Used by permission of Tyndale House Publishers, Inc.

Scripture quotations taken from the New Century Version (NCV). Copyright © 2005 by Thomas Nelson, Inc. Used by permission. All rights reserved.

Scripture quotations marked TPT are from The Passion Translation®. Copyright © 2017, 2018, 2020 by Passion & Fire Ministries, Inc. Used by permission. All rights reserved. ThePassionTranslation.com.

Due to the changing nature of the internet, any web addresses, links, or URLs included in this publication may be changed or altered at any time. The author and publisher make no guarantee of its accessibility. The views and opinions expressed in this publication are solely those of the author.

Paperback ISBN: 979-8-9906475-0-3 | eBook ISBN: 979-8-9906475-1-0

Mike Prah LLC, Publisher, 12217 Distribution Pl., Beltsville, MD 20705

www.mikeprah.com | E-mail: info@mikeprah.com

Mike Prah LLC
We Make It Happen

This book is gratefully dedicated to my beloved Mama, Mildred Matilda Joe Kingston Richards.

Mama, your life exemplified unwavering love and tireless sacrifice. You were my superhero, keeping so many people safe in your arms. Your legacy of unwavering love and determination will live on. Thank you, Mama, for being the true matriarch of our family. Your legacy lives on. I really love you!

Purchase Information

This book may be purchased directly from the Author at www.carmeniagrant.com.

For bulk purchases, email the Author at carmeniagrant@krucrown.com.

Also available in paperback from many USA and international online retailers, including Amazon, Walmart, Barnes & Noble, Books-A-Million, and several online bookstores.

E-book versions such as Amazon Kindle, Apple Book, Barnes & Noble Nook, and Google E-book are available from the retailers above.

Contents

Acknowledgments	IX
HE Dressed Me — Poem	XI
Introduction	1
Chapter 1 — Back to the Beginning	5
Chapter 2 — My Desperate Escape Plan	13
Chapter 3 – Diapers to Now: Forever Partners	23
Chapter 4 — Everyday Kings	29
Chapter 5 — Our Genetic Code Echoes	35
Chapter 6 — He Hurts for Me	41
Chapter 7 — Love: It's Complicated But Simple	47
Chapter 8 — Father	55

Chapter 9 — Summary	59
A Word of Encouragement	63
Resources	67
Connect with Carmenia	69

Acknowledgments

I am deeply grateful to my parents and siblings, whose unwavering support and encouragement have been the bedrock of my journey in writing this book. Your love and belief in me have fueled my determination and inspired me to reach new heights.

Special thanks to Pastor Mike Prah, whose guidance, wisdom, and blessings have been instrumental in the writing and publishing of this book. Your mentorship has been a guiding light, leading me through every step of this creative process.

I extend my heartfelt appreciation to my spiritual father, Bishop Darlingston Johnson, whose teachings, prayers, and blessings have surrounded me with divine grace. Your presence in my life has been a source of strength and inspiration.

To the extraordinary men in my life who consistently make me feel cherished, supported, and special, your overflowing love has been an enduring source of indescribable joy. I am genuinely blessed to have you by my side.

Lastly, I express my deepest gratitude to my Heavenly Father. I am humbled and thankful to be a vessel you use to bring the love of Jesus to the world. I am honored to be called your child and friend. You are so special to me, and I love you so much, Father. Thank You!

HE Dressed Me — Poem

Once upon a time, I felt responsible and faulted,

The operation and mechanics of my mind crashed for a moment.

My thought process seemed one-sided and bare,

Leaving me feeling empty and alone,

Invisible and unnoticed.

Here I am, screams parting my lips,

I cried out, wanting to be noticed,

My feet selfishly tussling with the ground,

Attempting to part ways like Air Jordan in '95 and '96.

Here I am, don't you see me? I know you see me,

Physically and emotionally fractured,

Slowly succumbing to the harsh reality

Of my mind's inner workings.

It's true, I am invisible to him,

Not realizing that with HIM, I am invincible.

My Journal Excerpt

Today was slightly better, but still so hard. I made it through dialysis without any incident, which is something, I guess. I spent the afternoon looking through old photos, trying to remember the happier times. It's strange how memories can feel both comforting and painful. I keep wondering if I'll ever feel truly happy again. Sometimes, the weight of my own sadness scares me.

Introduction

Allow me to take you on a journey where, in His mercy, GOD transformed my life—a time when everything seemed to be going as planned (so I thought). Then, a surprising plot twist appeared, catching me off guard. As a sports fan, I recall the 2013 Iron Bowl, in which Alabama State only needed to kick a field goal to win. The kick fell short despite its length, allowing Auburn State to return it 100 yards to win the game.

Alabama stood on the field in disbelief, watching their opponents celebrate a victory they had assumed was theirs. Similarly, in 1995, the Knicks thought they had the game, only for Reggie Miller of the opposing Indiana Pacers to score back-to-back points, securing 8 points in 9 seconds and winning the game. That's exactly how I felt.

I believed I had completed every step expected of me as a child and into adulthood: high school, bachelor's and master's degrees, a prominent government job, and marriage to the love of my life, all before the age of 25. To me, everything seemed perfect: enjoy life and start a family two years later—that was the plan, and I was about to congratulate myself, "Like a girl, you did that." Then the unthinkable happened.

The stories in this book provide a glimpse into a time in my life when the oppressor (the devil) snatched victory from my grasp just as success seemed imminent. It describes a time when life threw significant challenges and disappointments at me, but God eventually delivered me to a place of purpose, love, and a fulfilling life. The Bible says,

"God saves those who suffer. Through their suffering, He gets them to listen through their pain. God is gently calling you from the jaws of trouble to an open place of freedom where He has set your table full of the best food" (Job 26:15-16, NCV).

Join me as I chronicle how I emerged from my trials, not broken but refined, not defeated but strengthened. Through all of the ups and downs, I'm convinced that the unrelenting storm was not a punishment but rather a means of preparing me for the manifestation of God's grand purpose in my life and the revelation of His unwavering love.

I believe my story can inspire your powerful comeback story. God *still* works miracles!

Chapter 1 — Back to the Beginning

Dad's Story

My Journal Excerpt

Today, I feel helpless. FATHER, where are you? Daddy did his best trying to cheer me up after divorce court. Today, I felt life draining from my body, especially during dialysis. This man said he doesn't want to be with me anymore. I passed out during dialysis. I want to just end it because look at me now. I look so ugly. Please let me sleep tonight and all day tomorrow so I won't remember anything. I just want to sleep for two days straight because I don't want to remember this day.

"What do you mean he's not coming back?" Daddy whispered, "That's what this letter is saying baby girl." His voice filled with disbelief. As I tried to process the broken promises, the weight of those words fell heavily on me. I searched for an explanation with tear-filled eyes, my voice trembling with confusion and desperation. "But Dad, he said he was going to grab some clothes, and he would be back. He promised he would stay with me forever." I pleaded, my voice breaking, hoping my world hadn't crumbled beneath my feet and that I was merely dreaming.

Daddy held me tightly, feeling my small and fragile body shake with each sob. He quietly told my mom, "My heart is aching for her, Rosey." Daddy often refers to Mommy as Rosey, his sweetheart. He continued, "It hasn't even been six months since we celebrated their marriage. Oh baby, everything is going to be alright," he said, feeling the pain of betrayal piercing his baby girl's heart. My husband and I had been committed to each other for over six years before standing in front of the Lord and our families. Our vow to always be there for one another no matter what happens now seems like distant echoes.

My head throbbed with an intensifying ache that was only matched by the swelling of my face from uncontrollable tears. At that moment, I could feel the weight of my pain being shared by two sets of Daddy's hands, nestled in his embrace, breathing heavily with frustration.

During that period, my Dad worked as an IT specialist and drove a van. Every morning before going to work, he would have his breakfast prepared by either my mother or himself. My mother is an excellent cook, but my Dad is no stranger to the kitchen. It is, in fact, his happy place. He breezed into the kitchen ahead of my mother, relishing the freedom to prepare whatever his appetite desired for the day. With his breakfast, computer bags, and other necessary items in hand, he would make his way to the doorway, closely followed by my mother, who always remembered something he needed but might have forgotten.

When he turned to say, "See you later, I love you, and have a blessed day," Rosey would be standing right there, holding something different each time. They would embrace and exchange heartfelt "I love yous," and then Dad would go about his day, doing what he loved best. My Daddy has a servant's heart, finding joy in serving others, whether it was his immediate or spiritual family in Christ.

Due to the abrupt change in circumstances that necessitated my undergoing numerous medical treatments, my dad's daily routine required adjustments.

Consequently, our mornings together—and yes, I mean 'our mornings'— Dad and his sweet yet annoying little girl (me), would ride together every morning as he dropped me off for treatment. I found myself back in my childhood environment, following the familiar routine.

You see, during my early school years, I purposefully included myself in my Dad's mornings by deliberately waking up late and relying on him to drive me to school. That ride was always accompanied by my Dad's loud, dreadful singing, embellished stories about how he wrestled bears with his bare hands in his youth, or pieces of advice that began with phrases like, 'There comes a time in your life ...' Let's say that nothing had changed.

Even though I had grown up and knew those stories were not true, Dad continued to tell them without missing a beat. As Dad drove me to treatment or any of my doctor's appointments, his singing became louder, and the stories became even more unbelievable, even though I knew they were not true as an adult. Unlike in the past, I genuinely looked forward to spending time with my Dad, relieving my mind of what would come in the next few minutes, as we lived about 15 minutes from the treatment center.

My Dad has a way of unintentionally preparing me for difficult days. For example, when I needed to go to court to finalize my divorce, he was the only one who accompanied me. "Baby girl, let's go!" he exclaimed. Despite my protests that I didn't want to go, he calmly replied, "Baby, you don't have a choice." Thinking I hadn't heard, he declared loudly, "I'm going to be with you, and we'll do what we have to do and come back home." I was already dressed and ready when he opened the door, but my face was swollen, and my eyes almost shut from crying all night.

On our way to face this dreaded day, the ride remained unchanged, except this time, I had to listen to Dad's stories of how he somehow managed to travel the entire continent of Africa, visit the Sahara Desert, and even fight a lion, all in a single day, before making it back home for dinner at 6:00 PM. But something was different this time.

His stories and singing did not last the entire journey. In fact, it was only a short time after he noticed my overwhelming and sad demeanor. Dad decided to listen to the radio and sing along with the music. Before I knew it, I was bobbing my head and snapping my fingers, and before long, I was singing so loudly that I forgot about the deep sadness I had felt all night and when we first got in the car.

I praise GOD for providing a present Dad. My Daddy has always been there for me, whether it was making my sister and me a special Valentine's Day dinner and setting the table like we were at a high-end restaurant or when I called him to cry during my freshman year of college after my first heartbreak, Daddy was always present. I was always a daddy's girl growing up. He would irritate my mother by taking on odd jobs around the house, such as building a shed that would take us forever to complete or assisting with my move at least once a year. Dad has always been present, and he continues to be.

So, it hurt even more to see my Dad's expression as I gave my testimony in divorce court. I felt like I had to be strong for him this time because his pain for me was visible on his face, especially when he dropped me off at the treatment center. My court date happened to coincide with my treatment. Daddy and I drove three hours back from court straight to treatment. I can truly say my Father God, graced me on that day, which still seems like yesterday.

To GOD, be all the glory for such a loving, caring, and present man, but most importantly, a man of GOD, my Dad.

Chapter 2 — My Desperate Escape Plan

Janvier's Story

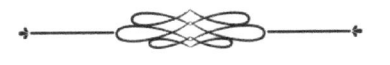

My Journal Excerpt

Today, mommy forced me to go for a walk. The sun was shining, and for a moment, it felt like it reached right into my soul. My body felt so good. My younger brother Janvier was slowly walking behind me just in case something were to happen as I am walking. Thank you FATHER, for my siblings. For some reason the sun felt so good that I didn't want to come back but I started to feel weak and Janvier slowly walked me back in the house.

Each morning, I woke up hoping that I was dreaming. The more I realized that this was now my reality, the more depression set in. I began to ask myself questions like, "Just like that? One minute, my life was going exactly as planned, and now there's so much uncertainty. How can this be? What did I do wrong?" I had just completed my master's degree and was in the process of applying for my doctoral psychology program. How could this happen to me? I had recently married the love of my life a few weeks after graduating and landed a job with the government, and now, all of this happened within a matter of months. How? What did I do wrong? These were questions I asked myself continuously up until recently.

Before falling ill, I was never known to be sick. So why now? What happened? I had many questions and asked my Father, GOD, day in and day out. I was in my early twenties. The more I asked these questions, the more alone I felt. Since I wasn't receiving any answers, I felt like there was only one thing left to do. I began planning my exit. I thought, "How can happiness be taken away just like that?"

Each day, I would plan, convinced it would work, but I was unsuccessful each time. Then, on one particular day, I had just received a three-month supply of my medications, and a lightbulb went off in my head. 'Yes,' I thought to myself. I even thanked God. That's how desperate I was. Dealing with both physical and mental pain was excruciating. Sleep felt like a luxury, especially at night. I was tormented by demonic spirits, making me feel worthless, like a nobody, especially after taking a shower at night and looking at my frail body in the mirror.

You see, before falling ill, I was chubby. I was the girl who was always on a diet but never able to lose a pound. I would publicly announce the start date of my diet and even invite others to join. The very next day, someone would happen to make my favorite meal, and guess what? My start date would change. Now that I was losing weight so rapidly, even size zero was too big for me. The devil began playing mind games with me, and I couldn't even find a permanent home for the depression in my mind. I felt like I was nobody, walking in shame and embarrassment.

The thought of getting married to the love of my life, two families coming together to start our own, only to have it all snatched away within a matter of months felt like death. I thought that the devil had stolen an entire family from me.

Not only did my husband at the time abandon me, but his entire family also ended a seven-year relationship abruptly. I had no hope, sick and abandoned by my husband. At the time, I felt like I had nothing to live for.

A particular plan came to mind as I searched for many ways to exit this world a little faster. I poured out a handful of most of the three-month supply of my medication and realized that I didn't have water. Just then, my brother, Janvier, walked into the room to check on me, as he always did. I hid my hand behind my back, not wanting him to see what was in my hand. I asked, "Could you get me a bottle of water?" He responded, "Sure, sis." As he went up the stairs, I gathered more medications, this time mixing them to make them more effective. He came down with the water and started talking. To this day, I don't know what he was talking about. The man couldn't stop talking. He talked and talked, and all I could think was, "Can he stop talking and leave?" But the more I wished he would leave, the more he continued to talk.

The longer he talked, the more the medication began to melt away. Janvier spoke for over an hour, and those who know Janvier know that he doesn't talk much. But that day was different.

That night, as all was silent, I thought, 'Here comes another long night of torment from the adversary, known as the devil,' which caused me to start sleeping with the lights on. As I lay in my bed, I realized I hadn't turned on the bathroom light, so I got out of bed to turn it on. Just as I laid back down, I clearly heard a loud whisper of Isaiah 54. I quickly dismissed it and took two Tylenol PM to fall asleep faster. All through the night, as I slept, I repeatedly heard Isaiah 54 so loudly. It took me some time to realize that I needed to find and read the Scripture. Tears filled my eyes uncontrollably as I opened the Bible and began to read the passage. The story was about me. GOD, my FATHER, started speaking:

"Sing, O childless woman, you who have never given birth!

Break into loud and joyful song, O Jerusalem,

you who have never been in labor.

For the desolate woman now has more children

than the woman who lives with her husband," says the Lord.

2 "Enlarge your house; build an addition.

Spread out your home and spare no expense!

3 For you will soon be bursting at the seams.

Your descendants will occupy other nations

and resettle the ruined cities.

4 Fear not; you will no longer live in shame.

Don't be afraid; there is no more disgrace for you.

You will no longer remember the shame of your youth

and the sorrows of widowhood.

5 For your Creator will be your husband;

the Lord of Heaven's Armies is his name!

He is your Redeemer, the Holy One of Israel,

the God of all the earth.

6 For the Lord has called you back from your grief—

as though you were a young wife abandoned by her husband," says your God.

7 "For a brief moment I abandoned you,

but with great compassion I will take you back.

8 In a burst of anger I turned my face away for a little while.

But with everlasting love, I will have compassion on you,"

says the Lord, your Redeemer.

9 "Just as I swore in the time of Noah

that I would never again let a flood cover the earth,

so now I swear that I will never again be angry and punish you.

10 For the mountains may move and the hills disappear,

but even then, my faithful love for you will remain.

My covenant of blessing will never be broken,"

says the Lord, who has mercy on you.

11 "O storm-battered city, troubled and desolate!

I will rebuild you with precious jewels

and make your foundations from lapis lazuli.

12 I will make your towers of sparkling rubies,

your gates of shining gems,

and your walls of precious stones.

13 I will teach all your children,

and they will enjoy great peace.

14 You will be secure under a government

that is just and fair.

Your enemies will stay far away.

You will live in peace,

and terror will not come near.

15 If any nation comes to fight you,

it is not because I sent them.

Whoever attacks you will go down in defeat.

16 "I have created the blacksmith

who fans the coals beneath the forge

and makes the weapons of destruction.

And I have created the armies that destroy.

17 But in that coming day,

no weapon turned against you will succeed.

You will silence every voice raised up to accuse you.

These benefits are enjoyed by the servants of the Lord;

their vindication will come from me.

I, the Lord, have spoken! – (Isaiah 54, NLT).

FATHER, you love me, I repeated with the biggest smile that turned into sobbing.

I give thanks to God for my younger big brother, Janvier. No matter how much I get on his last nerves – and I do – it's for good reasons. I know he's one of my biggest cheerleaders. I am blessed that he will always be there for his big sister, Jahmina, aka Me.

My Journal Excerpt

> I had a dream last night that felt so real. We were all together, laughing and happy. Waking up to the sound of the small heater in my room and the soft noise in my parents' home as they all got ready for school and work. I miss feeling connected to the outside world and to others. Hopefully one of my cousins will stop by. It's always so much laughter and fun when they're around. They somehow make me forget what's going on.

Chapter 3 – Diapers to Now: Forever Partners

Big Bro Amazing: Ronnie

Journal Entry

This morning, I woke up feeling a bit more energy than usual and somehow less ashamed. I don't know but maybe it's a sign that things are going to change soon. I don't know... my quite time with you was less tearful. I still have this nervous feeling in my stomach though. Please take it away FATHER. Maybe it will be much better after tomorrow's quiet time with you. Today big brother Amazing didn't stop by, but we talked for a long time over the phone and it was so peaceful. Thank you, FATHER, for my angel on earth. I'm grateful for him.

Why are you so sad? I asked as I was not used to seeing him like this. I continued to inquire with a trembling voice but still received no answer. When I noticed his eyes were beginning to water, I burst into tears and asked him, "What's wrong?" He replied, "You know I would give my life for you, right?"

As I cried, I said, "Yes, I know this with all my heart." He expressed his frustration with himself. He went on to say that every time he went to the hospital for additional tests regarding donating a kidney, his blood pressure would rise to an unhealthy level. However, when he got home, it was normal. The doctor warned him not to take the risk, even though he was a match. This was the final round of testing, and he was no longer eligible to donate.

My oldest brother and I share an unexplainable and timeless bond. I often joke that the Lord, in His wisdom, knew I needed an angel on earth in the flesh, so He gave me my amazing big brother—a perfectly packaged gift for me.

I needed Ronnie to be my big brother in this life. We formed a strong bond through shared memories, laughter, and major challenges. Ronnie has been my protector and guide since I was born, and he takes pride in encouraging and supporting me.

My "Big Brother Amazing" has always been a man of high standards, a natural leader who takes pride in his position as the oldest without saying so. He's the first of six. As the eldest, he never used his birthright to command respect from my younger siblings and me. Big Brother leads with humility and respects people regardless of age.

He demonstrates his leadership abilities not only within our family but also in the community. He is a brother, uncle, father figure, and friend to many people. His most important role is a father to my nephew-son and niece-daughter. He is a true gift, and I can honestly say that our Father, God, created him for this purpose.

The year was 2008. Given the sudden and unexpected change in my life, this is when life dealt me a hand I did not expect. I was now living with my parents and going to treatment three days a week. Nights were dreadful. I was afraid of being alone after everyone had gone to their rooms to rest for the night. Demonic forces tormented me at night, making me scared to close my eyes and sleep. As a result, I would stay up all night, further compromising my health. After I mentioned the problem to my oldest brother, he came up with a potential solution.

Instead of going home after work, Big Bro, as always, would spend the night with me to ensure I got enough rest. Sometimes, he would stay with me during the week after work and return home early the following day to prepare for work. My parents and I began to notice that "Big Brother Amazing" was exhausted from a lack of sleep. We tried to persuade him to sleep at home and come on weekends, but he refused.

One day, I reached a breaking point and realized I couldn't take the torment any longer. Overwhelmed by desperation, I began to cry out to God, pleading for relief from the nighttime anguish that had held me captive for far too long. The weight of my suffering had reached a point where tears would flow in the stillness of the night as I yearned for some semblance of peace. Recognizing how much toll it took on myself and those I cared about, I implored my Father, El Roi, the God who sees everything. In His mercy, He set me free that day.

"Big Brother Amazing" began noticing positive changes in my sleep patterns, prompting him to spend more nights at his own home as my newfound peace became apparent. This isn't just for me or his family; Big Brother is amazing and has a heart for others. He is a man of great integrity and compassion. Big Brother enjoys making people feel comfortable, appreciated, and good about themselves.

After three months of adjusting to dialysis treatment and the physical toll it takes, I finally agreed, as my mother begged me to go to church. I didn't want to go to church and face the embarrassment and questions that people had.

Not only was I dealing with a life-threatening illness, but my husband had left me and filed for legal separation. I, too, was trying to make sense of the situation. I was depressed and broke, having spent everything I had on a lavish wedding just a few months before. I didn't have any answers for myself, let alone others. I felt shameful and unattractive. I didn't want to leave the room for those visiting, so leaving the house was dreadful.

I stood in front of a full closet with nothing to wear. Now, this was a reality. Before becoming ill, I had a closet full of beautiful clothes and shoes. I even had the nickname "shoes" given to me by my cousins at one time. But I would still find an excuse to buy more, claiming I had nothing to wear (a common female problem). This time, standing in front of the closet was an actual reality. I was down more than 30 pounds from my normal weight of 140 pounds.

As I stood there feeling sorry for myself, "Big Brother Amazing" arrived with two bags. One has the most beautiful green and tan dress I've ever seen, and the other has a brown pair of the most beautiful and expensive shoes I've ever worn.

He stood in the doorway, smiling from ear to ear. "Big Brother Amazing" went to the store and independently chose both the dress and shoes. I wondered, 'How did he know my new dress and shoe size?' I had shrunk so much that everything hung off my frail body. Surprisingly, Big Brother had also planned for my cousin to do my hair. As you can see, the name "Big Brother Amazing" suits him perfectly.

A brother's love often goes beyond words, manifesting in encouraging gestures, shared glances that speak volumes without saying anything, and a dedication to each other's well-being. Whether we're having fun or dealing with difficulties, my oldest brother, Ronnie, believes that love provides a sense of security and belonging. This bond demonstrates that even as we change and grow older, the love between my big brother and me remains strong and enduring.

I love you so much, Ronnie, aka my Big Brother Amazing. I give our Father, God, all the glory for you!

Chapter 4 — Everyday Kings

Kings Men

My Journal Excerpt

Today, I am meeting with the doctors to go over my lab results. I'm so nervous. I can't sleep, and I'm shaking as if I have a fever. I keep using the bathroom. I can't keep anything down. GOD, help me. I know YOU told me not to be afraid, but it's hard. I didn't sleep last night because I am so scared. GOD, help me. Now, I feel like throwing up because I am so scared. GOD, help me.

In this particular season of my life, I found myself dealing with betrayal and abandonment from those I cared about. The pain was, at times, overwhelming, causing me to withdraw from others. I always told myself, "I don't need them; I have the Holy Spirit, also known as my best friend." Little did I know that divine intervention would soon challenge this viewpoint.

During this emotional turmoil, I began dialysis treatment three days a week, with each session lasting three hours. Furthermore, my mother's insistence on a strict plant-based diet created both novelty and financial strain. Organic markets became our regular haunt, with a single paper bag of groceries costing more than $100. The situation appeared hopeless until two unsung heroes, Uncle Ben and Uncle Sam, emerged from our tight-knit church community.

Our relationship with Harvest Intercontinental spans over thirty years, and these generous souls have been a part of it for the same time, if not longer. Our church had a large congregation, but the bonds were tight. Their dedication was unwavering, and they stepped up when they saw my family's need. The need was unassuming yet vital – a weekly supply of fresh fruits and vegetables for consumption and juicing.

Uncle Ben, knowing my dietary restrictions, carefully selected farm-fresh produce. Meanwhile, Uncle Sam, a man of action, delivered the bounty to my door and expertly transformed it into nutritious juices that kept me going for days. This became a weekly showcase of their selflessness and dedication.

In the midst of this health crisis, humor found its place. Uncle Sam would sometimes forget to wash the vegetables before juicing them. A gentle reminder from me would be met with Uncle Sam's soothing words, "It's okay, my child; the dirt will help heal your body." Perplexed, I'd exchange glances with him, and as we both burst out laughing, he'd repeat, "The dirt will help heal your body." This lighthearted banter became an essential part of our daily routine, lasting until a few months before my kidney transplant.

Then comes my church "Big Bro."

"Sis, this powerful man of God is coming to town, and I would love for us to visit. I've heard of numerous healings taking place during his services. Could you ask Aunty Rose and Uncle Llew (my parents) if I could take you?"

Before I could say anything, he added, "You know what? I will ask them myself. He abruptly ended the call without allowing me to respond, saying, 'I'll call them right away." The sequence of him contacting me, proposing the idea, almost seeking permission, and making the decision on his own, all while leaving me speechless, was not entirely unexpected. Adolphus Walker is one of my big brothers from church.

Adolphus has a passion for music and has been the choir director since I was in middle school. I looked forward to him picking me up in his black Acura Legend for choir practice on Saturdays or Sunday mornings for church because I knew it would be a fun ride with the other choir members. We developed a strong big brother-small sister family bond over the years, and he was always looking out for me.

The day had come to attend the church service that the man of God had visited. 'Sis, are you ready?' With no response from me, he yelled up the stairs, 'Sis, hurry up; we're running late. It is a three-hour drive. Running late as usual, I dashed down the stairs, still putting on my earrings and finishing up my hair, and asked, "What do you mean three hours?" Where are we going? He stated, 'The guy is in New York.' I told myself, 'This is love.' I thank God for blessing me with incredible people who went above and beyond to ensure my well-being.

These remarkable men of God are part of a community beyond the church walls. Their actions were motivated not by our requests but by an innate sense of solidarity. Their steadfast support eased the burden of a difficult season and illuminated the path the Lord had set for me. Uncle Ben, Uncle Sam, and Adolphus are Kingsmen who exemplified the spirit of community and love during a time when I most needed it.

Chapter 5 — Our Genetic Code Echoes

Aubrey's Story

"Cousin, cousin, we're a perfect match. We match in every way you can imagine within your body." As he shouted joyfully, my legs grew weak, and my lips trembled, ready for tears to flow. I asked, "What have you done? What have you done, Breezy?"

Then it crossed my mind: Could this be a prank? When the phone went silent, he began to yell, "HELLO! Did you hear me? I've been tested, and we're a match!" Overwhelmed, I cried out, "Tell me again. Please, say it again," as tears streamed down my face. The ecstatic screams transformed into a confident tone. "Yo, I'm serious, cousin. You will live. GOD will use me for you to live. I promised I would make it happen, and now we're a match." I dropped the phone and broke into loud sobs, forgetting I was at work. My colleagues rushed in, concerned, to find out what was going on. In that office, we were like a family. They all joined in the celebration when they found out why I was sobbing so hard.

Here is how it all began . . .

We were at one of our two hangout spots on this day, having so much fun doing absolutely nothing. The first was Sister EB's house, and the second was Sam's. We spent most of our days at either of these places, where we would cook, eat, play games, tell stories, or just clown around. We all had jobs, but our work schedules seemed to coincide because we were all at one of the two hangout spots on the same day and time. This hangout group consisted of cousins and friends who have become family to this day. We were very close. We even thought we were a rap/singing group at one point.

I had dialysis treatment three days a week on Monday, Wednesday, and Friday during this period. This group took turns driving me to treatment. Breezy volunteered to take me to treatment on this particular day. When we arrived at the treatment center, Breezy chose to remain in the car while I reluctantly walked into the dialysis center, thinking to myself, "LORD, I don't want to deal with the needles, the cramping, possibly passing out today." I quickly erased the thought, knowing that this was how my blood would be cleaned, increasing my chances of living.

After being hooked to the machine, I prepared for the three-hour procedure. My treatment lasted for about three hours. I would usually watch TV, listen to a sermon, music, or sleep during this time. That day, I decided to watch TV. As I searched my purse for my headphones, I realized I left them in the car. I called Breezy immediately and asked him to bring my headphones, not thinking anything about his reaction.

He walked in, stood at the doorway, and froze. I heard one of the dialysis technicians asking, "Can I help you, sir?" Breezy did not respond. Again, she asked, "Can I help you, sir?" This time, he spoke to me, saying, "Yo, this is what you go through every week, CG?" he uttered loudly, tears streaming down his cheeks. CG is one of my many nicknames. I kept nodding, answering him with a look I still cannot describe. He walked in, placed his head next to mine, and whispered with tears still rolling down his face, "What can I do? I want to make sure you never come back here ever again. What can I do, cousin? Tell me, please."

"What's next, Ms. Loida?" Breezy inquired frantically. Ms. Loida was the case manager at Washington Hospital Center in Washington, D.C. Breezy became even more anxious as Ms. Loida explained that September would be best because they needed time to prepare me before scheduling a date for transplant. It was mid-July at the time. "What do you mean, September? Next week looks good to me, Ms. Loida; anything can happen to her before then," Breezy said.

"GOD, you're so faithful," I thought as I stood there. The date given in September was exactly two weeks before the finalization of my divorce. I am experiencing the love of God through my cousin Breezy. As these thoughts ran through my mind, I somehow snapped out of it and turned to him, saying, "Cousin, I want this as badly as you do, but I also understand what Ms. Loida is saying. We may not have a say in this part of the process. Let's wait patiently; GOD is in control."

Ms. Loida carefully explained the entire process, including the next steps. As we left Ms. Loida's office, Breezy started clapping firmly, saying, "Let's go, I've been ready like a week ago." As I rolled my eyes with a huge smile, I thought, "Yup, he's scared."

The big day finally arrived. "Are you okay, cousin? I asked. "You don't have to do this, blood." When something serious is about to go down, we refer to each other in this manner. "You don't have to," I said. Breezy replied, "We're family, and that's what family do." This is one of Breezy's famous sayings. Breezy is well-known in our family for having a big heart. He would fearlessly do anything for the people he loved, even if it meant risking his life. Everyone in our cousin's group can confirm this.

Soon after, the doctors came in to explain the day's process. Breezy turned to me as they talked and said, "I love you, CG. I would do anything for you, even give my life for you." About a year after the transplant, he had this saying, which included my name, tattooed on his arm.

The nurses came in and said it was time because he was the first to be wheeled into surgery. "See you and my kidney later, "blood"," he said, holding my hand and looking at my worried eyes.

Chapter 6 — He Hurts for Me
Bishop

"I'm not writing this to embarrass you or to shame you, but to correct you as the children I love. For although you could have countless babysitters in Christ telling you what you're doing wrong, you don't have many fathers who correct you in love. But I'm a true father to you, for I became your father when I gave you the gospel and brought you into union with Jesus, the Anointed One" (I Corinthians 4:14-15, TPT).

In my formative years, weekends revolved around activities at the church—Bible study, youth and young adult events, choir practice, and Sunday services. Bethel World Outreach Ministries, now Harvest Intercontinental Church Unlimited, was not just a church but a tight-knit community where my parents built a life. For my sibling and me, it wasn't just about close friends; our aunties, uncles, and cousins were also part of this fantastic group of people who love Jesus and each other, creating countless cherished memories as a church.

Even as I transitioned reluctantly from youth to the young adult ministry, I continued to serve in the choir and almost every ministry my parents and other siblings served in. The choir, my happy place as a child and even now as an adult, was where I found solace. Those were the days when the youth and young adults would embark on exciting trips across the country with our young and vibrant Bishop. The choir, which I believed to be the best in the world, would minister before Bishop preached, and our God would do his thing through His servants (us).

I remember one day in school when a friend was teasing and acting silly by imitating his pastor at church, and we all laughed. I quickly jumped up and said, "My pastor doesn't preach like that." They all looked at me strangely, saying,

'What are you talking about? All preachers preach like this." And I said, 'Maybe he's not a preacher, but he's like Mr. Daniels.' Mr. Daniels was one of our favorite teachers, a fun teacher who spoke to us with respect. He was a teacher who did not talk at us, but with us, ensuring we understood his lessons. Overall, Mr. Daniels was an amazing teacher. So, when I made the comparison to my Bishop, my best friend said, "I think I would like to come to your church instead of Grandma's." We all laughed and continued joking around.

Side note: my best friend ended up visiting my church, and it turned out Bishop was not there, and we had a guest preacher. Let's just say Monday morning on the school bus, the jokes started all over again.

Bishop's leadership is marked by thoughtfulness and genuine concern. What mattered to us mattered to him. His ability to remember all our names and notice if we missed a Sunday or two always left me in awe. Even when I was ill, he always asked me what the doctor said. I would be standing, and he would tell someone to get me a chair to sit without me knowing. Later, the person who brought the chair would say, "Bishop told me to get you a chair."

The day I was released from the hospital, after being transferred from Peninsula Regional Hospital in Salisbury, MD, to

Washington Hospital Center in Washington, DC, my parents drove me to the revival happening at our church that night. After the service, my parents and I were ushered upstairs to meet with the man of God for prayer. As we entered, Bishop Johnson commenced to inform the guest preacher about my current situation. He began by saying, "The upbringing of this young lady is deeply rooted in this church. She recently got married, and this has happened to her out of nowhere."

As my Bishop spoke with the man of God, I glanced at my spiritual father and was moved to tears. His eyes conveyed a mix of hurt and compassion, realizing that one of his own had encountered major adversity. While the men of God and my parents continued to converse regarding my case, I started thanking God as I found myself at peace for the first time since my diagnosis. I was in a familiar place again—a place of so much love, where people genuinely care for one another. A place I call home—my church home.

Our spiritual leader, Bishop Darlingston Johnson, demonstrates commitment beyond the pulpit as he actively engages with a diverse population, cultures, and needs, fostering unity and inclusivity. I strongly believe that over 90 percent of his grays came prematurely due to the responsibility of leading us, a responsibility that God has entrusted to him. Whether counseling individuals in personal struggles, praying for the sick, like he often did for me, or simply being there, Bishop Johnson's care extends beyond spiritual guidance. He is respected as a fantastic leader who loves Jesus and as a compassionate shepherd, exemplifying God's teachings of love, kindness, and service at the core.

Chapter 7 — Love: It's Complicated But Simple

As I embark on the journey of writing this chapter on love, a multitude of questions flood my mind. What, in essence, is love from my perspective? Why do individuals proclaim their love before God and a multitude of witnesses, only to see it crumble and fade away in the wake of transgressions? These ponderings impel me to delve deeper into the subject. Let's explore the insights from our "friend," Google.

Google initially recognizes love as both a noun and a verb—a fusion of sentiment and action. The first five definitions it presents are as follows:

An intense feeling of deep affection.

A great interest and pleasure in something.

A person or thing that one loves.

To feel deep affection for someone.

To like or enjoy something very much.

These definitions serve as the foundation for unraveling the complexities and nuances that love encompasses.

As profound as these definitions are, I wanted to go even deeper, this time by asking others for their personal perspectives on what love truly entails. Oh, boy, was I in for a surprise. Initially, I asked very close family and friends, and the responses ranged from playful banter to heartfelt revelations. Not satisfied with limiting my exploration to familiar faces, I expanded my search to include strangers. Here are the ten responses that stood out to me:

Love is an unwavering loyalty in good times or bad times.

Love is shown by being patient.

Love is freedom and does not keep score.

Love is reciprocity.

Love is meaningless because nobody means what they say.

Love is forgiveness.

Love is spiritual and cannot be explained.

Love is standing in power.

Love is long-suffering.

Remarkably, many refer to 1 Corinthians 13:4–8, which states, "Love is patient and kind; love does not envy or boast; it is not arrogant or rude. It does not insist on its own way; it is not irritable or resentful; it does not rejoice at wrongdoing but rejoices with the truth."

Some people were born into a traumatized world, while others grew up in single-parent households, missing both parents and the love that comes with them. Some have had the support of both parents and extended family, only to go through the unimaginable pain of molestation or abuse by close relatives. Others have never heard the simple but profound words "I love you" from a parent or family member.

I once met someone who shared a poignant experience with me. They revealed that they first heard the words "I love you" while in a romantic relationship. This revelation was a revelation unto itself. The individual admitted to struggling to respond, not knowing how to reciprocate, because it was their first exposure to those three powerful words. As a result, their lack of familiarity put their relationship in jeopardy. It occurred to me that many people, including this individual, had never heard those words and had no idea what it meant to express and receive love.

This realization significantly broadened my perspective and helped me comprehend the varied responses I had received when questioning others about the meaning of love. Each individual's opinion of love goes back to one thing. GOD.

GOD is Love, a profound truth supported by various scriptures that emphasize the divine nature of love.

According to 1 John 4:7-10, we are reminded to "love one another; everyone who loves has been born of God and knows God. Whoever does not love does not know God because God is love" (NIV).

John 3:16 further encapsulates this divine love, expressing that God's profound affection for the world led Him to give His Son, providing eternal life to those who believe in Him.

The pinnacle of love is depicted in John 15:13, where the willingness to lay down one's life for friends is deemed the greatest form of love.

These scriptures collectively form a solid foundation, revealing that God's love is selfless, sacrificial, and boundless. While scripture provides a comprehensive understanding of divine love, my personal experiences with the Lord enhance this comprehension and give me a more profound understanding of 1 Corinthians 13:4-8.

Let us now delve into 1 Corinthians 13:4-8, a chapter that intricately defines the attributes of love and provides a clearer understanding of its profound nature.

Love, as the scripture beautifully articulates, is patient. It is a deep reservoir of patience, refusing to succumb to frustration or abandon someone in the face of adversity. Instead, it remains unwavering and understanding amidst challenges.

Love is kind. It actively seeks opportunities to make a positive impact, treating others with compassion, gentleness, and a genuine desire to bring goodness into their lives.

Love does not envy. It comprehends that another's success or possessions do not diminish our worth. Rather than harboring jealousy, love celebrates the achievements and joys of those around us.

Love does not boast; it is humbling. It doesn't feel the need to showcase its accomplishments or prove its worth. Instead, it quietly and confidently engages in acts of goodness without seeking validation.

Love is not arrogant. It bears the mark of humility, avoiding any pretense of superiority and eschewing pride.

Love is not rude; it respects others. It involves politeness and avoidance of behaviors that may harm or offend.

Love does not insist on having its way. It embodies selflessness and flexibility, taking into account the needs and desires of others while also valuing mutual understanding and compromise.

Love is not irritable; it does not easily become angry or irritated. It keeps a calm and patient demeanor even under challenging situations.

Finally, love does not harbor resentment. True love does not keep a record of wrongdoings; rather, it practices forgiveness and avoids holding grudges. It rejoices in the truth rather than in wrongdoing.

This scripture paints a beautiful and comprehensive picture of love, emphasizing its selflessness, patience, and virtuous qualities.

Imagine a love so patient that it echoes Jesus' enduring compassion. This extraordinary love refuses to give up; its patience serves as a steadfast anchor, providing profound security in the face of life's challenges. It is the type of love that the heart desires, embracing understanding and acceptance. According to 1 John 4:18, such love is fearless because perfect love casts out all fear.

Envision a love that goes beyond mere kindness. It actively seeks opportunities to positively impact your life, whether through a thoughtful gesture from a friend, a mentor who encourages your dreams, or a family member who stands by you during difficult times. This selfless love gives without expecting anything in return.

These qualities of love are not distant ideals; they represent the love we all crave in our relationships, mirroring the love exemplified by Jesus.

Chapter 8 — Father

My Journal Excerpt

Holy Spirit, I felt YOUR presence so heavily. I could literally feel YOU around me. Its so hard to put the feeling I had into words. But I promised the therapist to put my feelings into words and I'm having a hard time because I feel like YOU came back as soon as I started writing this journal. I have this feeling of excitement and I can't stop smiling because I feel YOU'RE my new best friend.

I am deeply in love with You, understanding that You knew me intimately before I even comprehended myself. Taking Your time, You shaped me for Your pleasure, knowing every intricate detail about me, down to the number of strands on my head. You chose me to exist before the mere thought of me crossed my parents' mind. Sometimes, I find myself marveling at the mystery of who You are. Yet, in Your boundless mercy and love, You consistently reveal the facets of Yourself that I need and deeply long for.

Our moments together are precious. I adore the way You love me, my Father—a love I know I don't deserve yet feel every single day. Even when I was oblivious to Your existence, You cared for me. You shared in every heartbreak, endured every moment of my shame, abuse, and pain, never once leaving me alone, even though I was unaware of Your presence. I was disconnected and unaware of when You were near. Even during the times I knowingly and unknowingly hurt You through my disobedience, You consistently remained by my side. Your presence is constant, unwavering, and forever.

I'm not proud of the mistakes that caused me to hurt You, but You don't push me aside. Instead, You hold me close and guide me back on track. Your watchful care began in my mother's womb (Jeremiah 1:5), shielding me from the enemy who sought to claim me. You declared, "Not this one."

My life has a purpose beyond just populating the earth; You crafted me for a specific assignment, a purpose You've revealed to me in Your mercy.

Father, time and again, You've shielded and preserved me. In Your mercy, You've illuminated my purpose. Although the how may elude me, it is not mine to worry about. I trust You have it all planned out, preparing me for the appointed time when it will come to fruition. Your goodness overwhelms me, and I often ponder if You fully grasp the depth of Your own goodness. Father, You have chosen me, and I chose You back. Having a relationship with You is life itself, and You, my Father, are my life.

Chapter 9 — Summary

In the midst of life's trials, it often felt like a never-ending storm, with questions of "why me" and moments of doubting God's love resonating in my mind. It was a difficult journey that seemed to lack purpose and divine intervention. In those moments of despair, I failed to recognize that this was a set-up, a divine orchestration directing me toward the fulfillment of my destiny.

Little did I realize that the hardships were not punishments but rather stepping stones to a greater goal. This intricate tapestry of challenges reminded me of Jeremiah 29:11. "I know the thoughts that I think toward you, says the LORD, thoughts of peace, and not of evil, to give you an expected end."

Suddenly, the pieces fell into place, and I realized that my struggles were not an indication of divine abandonment but rather the beginning of a remarkable transformation. In His infinite wisdom, God was shaping a narrative beyond my comprehension—one of hope and a future that transcended the setbacks I faced.

Through the lens of faith, I began to see how, even in the darkest of times, God was working tirelessly behind the scenes to transform adversity into a testimony to His unwavering love and purpose for my life. Each trial and setback was a thread meticulously woven into the grand design of my story, a story of resilience and redemption.

In retrospect, I could see divine fingerprints on every stage of my life. The seemingly never-ending storms helped shape me into the person I was meant to be. God's plan unfolded in ways I could not have predicted, and the difficulties were not stumbling blocks but stepping stones to fulfilling His promise.

As I accepted this new perspective, my faith grew stronger. Previously perceived as aimless, the journey now had a profound sense of purpose. I understood that the seemingly unanswered prayers were part of a divine strategy to guide me to a destiny far more magnificent than I had ever imagined.

By trusting the process, I discovered that God's love was not confined to my moments of joy but extended into the depths of my struggles. The narrative of my life, written by the Author of all things, unfolded gracefully, turning what seemed like a chaotic tale into a masterpiece of faith and endurance.

So, as the storm clouds dispersed, I emerged from the trials not broken but refined, not defeated but strengthened. Through the twists and turns, the highs and lows, I realized that the relentless storm was not a punishment but a prelude to the revelation of God's unwavering love and the manifestation of His purpose in my life.

So, as the storm clouds cleared, I emerged from my trials, not broken but refined, not defeated but strengthened. Through the twists and turns, the highs and lows, I realized that the relentless storm was not a punishment, but rather a preparation for the revelation of God's unwavering love and the manifestation of His grand purpose in my life. Hallelujah!

A Word of Encouragement

A Letter from a Loving Friend

Hi Friend,

It's unimaginable what you're going through, and I want to extend my heartfelt support to you during this incredibly tough time.

First and foremost, please know that you are not alone. Many people care about you and are ready to help you through this. It's completely natural to feel overwhelmed by such significant life changes and health challenges, but there is hope and a way forward.

I understand that things might seem insurmountable right now, but I encourage you to hold onto hope. Life can bring unexpected joys even in the midst of our darkest hours. Remember, your strength in Jesus is greater than any obstacle in your path—even when it doesn't feel that way.

In times like these, it's important to lean on your faith, because the Word of God says when we're weak, He is strong. You're not alone. Trust that the Holy Spirit is with you, even if you don't understand it all. Allow Him to be your comfort. You don't have to face this alone. There is an entire community waiting to help you, and there are professionals who can provide you with the care and support you need to navigate this time. Please consider reaching out to a therapist or counselor.

Your life is precious, and your story isn't over. There are new chapters ahead, new joys to be found, and new strengths to be gained. I believe God will get you through this because you are stronger than you think. Take each day at a time and allow yourself the grace to feel what you need to feel.

Finally, hold onto the fact that there is always a possibility for new beginnings and healing. You are capable of navigating this difficult period and emerging with new resilience. Your journey may be tough, but it will also be filled with moments of hope and light—Jesus.

With all my love and support.

Resources

Centers for Disease Control and Prevention, National Center for Injury Prevention and Control

---

If you or someone you know is struggling or in crisis, help is available.

Call or text 988 or chat 988lifeline.org

Contact the 988 Suicide and Crisis Lifeline if you are experiencing mental health-related distress or are worried about a loved one who may need crisis support.

Call or text 988

Chat at 988lifeline.org

Connect with a trained crisis counselor. 988 is confidential, free, and available 24/7/365.

Visit the 988 Suicide and Crisis Lifeline for more information at 988lifeline.org

Abuse/Assault/Violence

National Domestic Violence Hotline: 1-800-799-7233 or text LOVEIS to 22522

National Child Abuse Hotline: 1-800-4AChild (1-800-422-4453) or text 1-800-422-4453

National Sexual Assault Hotline: 1-800-656-HOPE (4673) or Online Chat

Disaster Distress Helpline: CALL or TEXT 1-800-985-5990 (press 2 for Spanish)

Connect with Carmenia

www.krucrown.com

Email: carmeniagrant@krucrown.com

At KruCrown, we recognize that your hair isn't just strands—it reflects your identity, confidence, and journey. It's your covering, your glory (1 Corinthians 11:15). That's why we're committed to offering more than just natural hair care products; we provide a sanctuary for both your hair and soul.

KruCrown was born from my personal battle with a life-threatening illness, during which my hair became a testament to my faith, embodying both my strength and my path to healing. I know firsthand the importance of caring for your scalp and hair, especially during challenging times.

We specialize in scalp and hair wellness services for women who, like me, once faced or are facing life-threatening illnesses, trauma, or mental illness that result in hair loss. Our mission is to help you regain your hair, nurture your spirit, and restore your confidence.

With KruCrown, you're not just a client; you're a part of our family. Join us on this journey of healing and self-discovery because your hair deserves the very best care, and so do you.

Visit www.krucrown.com

Be Bold, Be Confident, Be You!